Everyone was excited. It was half-term.
"For homework," said Mrs May. "I'd like you to keep an autumn diary."
"Oh no!" said Biff. "Homework!"

Chip phoned Gran.

"We can't stay with you all week," he said. "We've got to keep a nature diary. It's homework."

"Don't worry," Gran replied. "We can get the homework done and have some fun."

The next day, Dad took Biff and Chip to Gran's. They picked up Nadim on the way. He was going too.

"It will be fun at Gran's," said Biff.
"I know," said Nadim. "But when will we get time to write our nature diary?"

They got to Gran's, but she didn't come to the door.

"How odd!" said Dad. "She knows we are coming. Let's look in the garden."

There were lots of things in the garden. "How odd!" said Biff. "Why has Gran put sunbeds out? It's not summer."

Suddenly, Gran opened the door of the shed.

"Surprise!" she said.

The children looked inside.

They all gasped.

"I've made a nature laboratory," said Gran. "We can do the nature project in here. It will be fun."

Gran took the children into the woods.
"Let's start with the trees," she said.
They collected lots of different leaves.

Gran gave Nadim paper and crayons.
"Put the paper against the tree. Then rub the crayon over it," she said. "It's called a bark rubbing."

Back in the laboratory, they looked at the bark rubbings.

"Each type of tree has a different bark," said Nadim.

They stuck the leaves in their diaries. Gran had seeds from the trees.

"We'll plant these in pots," she said. "One day they will grow into trees."

The next morning Gran got up early. She mixed seeds and nuts with melted fat and poured it into little pots.

"What is that smell?" asked Chip.

"Breakfast!" said Gran.

"I don't want to eat that!" said Biff.

"It's not for you!" said Gran. "It's for the birds!"

When the fat had set in the pots,
Gran hung them in the garden.
"We can watch the birds," she said.

In the afternoon, Gran took them to a special place in the woods.

"Now for a secret," said Gran. "Look!"

The children looked around. There were coloured mushrooms everywhere.
"Its amazing!" gasped Nadim.
"Look, but don't touch," said Gran.

On the way home Chip found some marks in the mud.

"Are they animal tracks?" he asked.

Gran got some powder out of her bag. She mixed it with water and made a paste. Then she poured the paste on to the animal track.

"This is plaster," said Gran. "It will dry in the shape of the animal track. It's called a cast."

They took the cast back to the laboratory. Biff looked up the animal track in a book.

"It's from a badger," she said.

"Tonight I have another surprise," said Gran. "We need to wrap up warm and we'll need the sunbeds."

"Sunbeds?" asked Biff.

They lay on the sunbeds and looked up. The sky was full of shooting stars.

"This is amazing!" said Chip.

"And it's your homework!" said Gran.